Name It!

The Little Book For Character Names

Created & Designed By
TeeCee Design Studio

Character Name

Also Known By

In Which Book Used

Major/Minor Character

Age

Height

Weight

Build

Eye Color

Hair Color

Hair Style

Distinguishing Marks

Extra Notes

Character Name

Eye Color

Also Known By

Hair Color

In Which Book Used

Hair Style

Major/Minor Character

Distinguishing Marks

Age

Height

Extra Notes

Weight

Build

| Character Name | Eye Color |

| Also Known By | Hair Color |

| In Which Book Used | Hair Style |

| Major/Minor Character | Distinguishing Marks |

| Age | |

| Height | Extra Notes |

| Weight | |

| Build | |

Character Name

Also Known By

In Which Book Used

Major/Minor Character

Age

Height

Weight

Build

Eye Color

Hair Color

Hair Style

Distinguishing Marks

Extra Notes

Character Name

Also Known By

In Which Book Used

Major/Minor Character

Age

Height

Weight

Build

Eye Color

Hair Color

Hair Style

Distinguishing Marks

Extra Notes

Character Name

Also Known By

In Which Book Used

Major/Minor Character

Age

Height

Weight

Build

Eye Color

Hair Color

Hair Style

Distinguishing Marks

Extra Notes

Character Name

Also Known By

In Which Book Used

Major/Minor Character

Age

Height

Weight

Build

Eye Color

Hair Color

Hair Style

Distinguishing Marks

Extra Notes

Character Name

Also Known By

In Which Book Used

Major/Minor Character

Age

Height

Weight

Build

Eye Color

Hair Color

Hair Style

Distinguishing Marks

Extra Notes

Character Name

Also Known By

In Which Book Used

Major/Minor Character

Age

Height

Weight

Build

Eye Color

Hair Color

Hair Style

Distinguishing Marks

Extra Notes

Character Name

Eye Color

Also Known By

Hair Color

In Which Book Used

Hair Style

Major/Minor Character

Distinguishing Marks

Age

Height

Extra Notes

Weight

Build

Character Name

Also Known By

In Which Book Used

Major/Minor Character

Age

Height

Weight

Build

Eye Color

Hair Color

Hair Style

Distinguishing Marks

Extra Notes

Character Name	Eye Color

Also Known By	Hair Color

In Which Book Used	Hair Style

Major/Minor Character	Distinguishing Marks

Age

Height

Weight

Build

Extra Notes

Character Name

Eye Color

Also Known By

Hair Color

In Which Book Used

Hair Style

Major/Minor Character

Distinguishing Marks

Age

Height

Extra Notes

Weight

Build

Character Name

Also Known By

In Which Book Used

Major/Minor Character

Age

Height

Weight

Build

Eye Color

Hair Color

Hair Style

Distinguishing Marks

Extra Notes

Character Name	Eye Color

Also Known By	Hair Color

In Which Book Used	Hair Style

Major/Minor Character	Distinguishing Marks

Age

Height

Weight

Build

Extra Notes

Character Name

Also Known By

In Which Book Used

Major/Minor Character

Age

Height

Weight

Build

Eye Color

Hair Color

Hair Style

Distinguishing Marks

Extra Notes

Character Name

Also Known By

In Which Book Used

Major/Minor Character

Age

Height

Weight

Build

Eye Color

Hair Color

Hair Style

Distinguishing Marks

Extra Notes

Character Name

Also Known By

In Which Book Used

Major/Minor Character

Age

Height

Weight

Build

Eye Color

Hair Color

Hair Style

Distinguishing Marks

Extra Notes

Character Name

Also Known By

In Which Book Used

Major/Minor Character

Age

Height

Weight

Build

Eye Color

Hair Color

Hair Style

Distinguishing Marks

Extra Notes

Character Name

Also Known By

In Which Book Used

Major/Minor Character

Age

Height

Weight

Build

Eye Color

Hair Color

Hair Style

Distinguishing Marks

Extra Notes

Character Name

Also Known By

In Which Book Used

Major/Minor Character

Age

Height

Weight

Build

Eye Color

Hair Color

Hair Style

Distinguishing Marks

Extra Notes

Character Name

Also Known By

In Which Book Used

Major/Minor Character

Age

Height

Weight

Build

Eye Color

Hair Color

Hair Style

Distinguishing Marks

Extra Notes

Character Name

Also Known By

In Which Book Used

Major/Minor Character

Age

Height

Weight

Build

Eye Color

Hair Color

Hair Style

Distinguishing Marks

Extra Notes

Character Name

Also Known By

In Which Book Used

Major/Minor Character

Age

Height

Weight

Build

Eye Color

Hair Color

Hair Style

Distinguishing Marks

Extra Notes

Character Name

Also Known By

In Which Book Used

Major/Minor Character

Age

Height

Weight

Build

Eye Color

Hair Color

Hair Style

Distinguishing Marks

Extra Notes

Character Name

Also Known By

In Which Book Used

Major/Minor Character

Age

Height

Weight

Build

Eye Color

Hair Color

Hair Style

Distinguishing Marks

Extra Notes

Character Name	Eye Color

Character Name

Eye Color

Also Known By

Hair Color

In Which Book Used

Hair Style

Major/Minor Character

Distinguishing Marks

Age

Height

Extra Notes

Weight

Build

Character Name

Also Known By

In Which Book Used

Major/Minor Character

Age

Height

Weight

Build

Eye Color

Hair Color

Hair Style

Distinguishing Marks

Extra Notes

Character Name

Also Known By

In Which Book Used

Major/Minor Character

Age

Height

Weight

Build

Eye Color

Hair Color

Hair Style

Distinguishing Marks

Extra Notes

Character Name

Also Known By

In Which Book Used

Major/Minor Character

Age

Height

Weight

Build

Eye Color

Hair Color

Hair Style

Distinguishing Marks

Extra Notes

Character Name	Eye Color

Also Known By	Hair Color

In Which Book Used	Hair Style

Major/Minor Character	Distinguishing Marks

Age	

Height	Extra Notes

Weight	

Build	

Character Name

Eye Color

Also Known By

Hair Color

In Which Book Used

Hair Style

Major/Minor Character

Distinguishing Marks

Age

Height

Weight

Extra Notes

Build

Character Name

Eye Color

Also Known By

Hair Color

In Which Book Used

Hair Style

Major/Minor Character

Distinguishing Marks

Age

Height

Extra Notes

Weight

Build

Character Name	Eye Color

Also Known By	Hair Color

In Which Book Used	Hair Style

Major/Minor Character	Distinguishing Marks

Age

Height

Weight

Build

Extra Notes

Character Name

Eye Color

Also Known By

Hair Color

In Which Book Used

Hair Style

Major/Minor Character

Distinguishing Marks

Age

Height

Extra Notes

Weight

Build

Character Name

Also Known By

In Which Book Used

Major/Minor Character

Age

Height

Weight

Build

Eye Color

Hair Color

Hair Style

Distinguishing Marks

Extra Notes

Character Name

Also Known By

In Which Book Used

Major/Minor Character

Age

Height

Weight

Build

Eye Color

Hair Color

Hair Style

Distinguishing Marks

Extra Notes

Character Name

Also Known By

In Which Book Used

Major/Minor Character

Age

Height

Weight

Build

Eye Color

Hair Color

Hair Style

Distinguishing Marks

Extra Notes

Character Name	Eye Color

Also Known By	Hair Color

In Which Book Used	Hair Style

Major/Minor Character	Distinguishing Marks

Age

Height

Weight

Build

Extra Notes

Character Name

Eye Color

Also Known By

Hair Color

In Which Book Used

Hair Style

Major/Minor Character

Distinguishing Marks

Age

Height

Extra Notes

Weight

Build

Character Name	Eye Color

Also Known By	Hair Color

In Which Book Used	Hair Style

Major/Minor Character	Distinguishing Marks

Age

Height

Weight

Build

Extra Notes

| Character Name | Eye Color |

| Also Known By | Hair Color |

| In Which Book Used | Hair Style |

| Major/Minor Character | Distinguishing Marks |

| Age |

| Height |

| Weight | Extra Notes |

| Build |

Character Name

Also Known By

In Which Book Used

Major/Minor Character

Age

Height

Weight

Build

Eye Color

Hair Color

Hair Style

Distinguishing Marks

Extra Notes

Character Name

Also Known By

In Which Book Used

Major/Minor Character

Age

Height

Weight

Build

Eye Color

Hair Color

Hair Style

Distinguishing Marks

Extra Notes

Character Name

Also Known By

In Which Book Used

Major/Minor Character

Age

Height

Weight

Build

Eye Color

Hair Color

Hair Style

Distinguishing Marks

Extra Notes

Character Name

Also Known By

In Which Book Used

Major/Minor Character

Age

Height

Weight

Build

Eye Color

Hair Color

Hair Style

Distinguishing Marks

Extra Notes

Character Name

Also Known By

In Which Book Used

Major/Minor Character

Age

Height

Weight

Build

Eye Color

Hair Color

Hair Style

Distinguishing Marks

Extra Notes

Character Name	Eye Color

Also Known By

In Which Book Used

Major/Minor Character

Age

Height

Weight

Build

Hair Color

Hair Style

Distinguishing Marks

Extra Notes

Character Name

Eye Color

Also Known By

Hair Color

In Which Book Used

Hair Style

Major/Minor Character

Distinguishing Marks

Age

Height

Extra Notes

Weight

Build

Character Name

Also Known By

In Which Book Used

Major/Minor Character

Age

Height

Weight

Build

Eye Color

Hair Color

Hair Style

Distinguishing Marks

Extra Notes

Character Name

Eye Color

Also Known By

Hair Color

In Which Book Used

Hair Style

Major/Minor Character

Distinguishing Marks

Age

Height

Extra Notes

Weight

Build

Character Name

Eye Color

Also Known By

Hair Color

In Which Book Used

Hair Style

Major/Minor Character

Distinguishing Marks

Age

Height

Weight

Extra Notes

Build

Character Name

Eye Color

Also Known By

Hair Color

In Which Book Used

Hair Style

Major/Minor Character

Distinguishing Marks

Age

Height

Extra Notes

Weight

Build

Character Name	Eye Color

Also Known By	Hair Color

In Which Book Used	Hair Style

Major/Minor Character	Distinguishing Marks

Age

Height

Weight

Build

Extra Notes

Character Name

Also Known By

In Which Book Used

Major/Minor Character

Age

Height

Weight

Build

Eye Color

Hair Color

Hair Style

Distinguishing Marks

Extra Notes

Character Name

Eye Color

Also Known By

Hair Color

In Which Book Used

Hair Style

Major/Minor Character

Distinguishing Marks

Age

Height

Weight

Extra Notes

Build

Character Name

Eye Color

Also Known By

Hair Color

In Which Book Used

Hair Style

Major/Minor Character

Distinguishing Marks

Age

Height

Extra Notes

Weight

Build

Character Name

Eye Color

Also Known By

Hair Color

In Which Book Used

Hair Style

Major/Minor Character

Distinguishing Marks

Age

Height

Extra Notes

Weight

Build

Character Name	Eye Color
Also Known By	Hair Color
In Which Book Used	Hair Style
Major/Minor Character	Distinguishing Marks
Age	
Height	Extra Notes
Weight	
Build	

Character Name

Also Known By

In Which Book Used

Major/Minor Character

Age

Height

Weight

Build

Eye Color

Hair Color

Hair Style

Distinguishing Marks

Extra Notes

Character Name	Eye Color

Also Known By	Hair Color

In Which Book Used	Hair Style

Major/Minor Character	Distinguishing Marks

Age

Height

Weight

Build

Extra Notes

Character Name

Also Known By

In Which Book Used

Major/Minor Character

Age

Height

Weight

Build

Eye Color

Hair Color

Hair Style

Distinguishing Marks

Extra Notes

Character Name

Also Known By

In Which Book Used

Major/Minor Character

Age

Height

Weight

Build

Eye Color

Hair Color

Hair Style

Distinguishing Marks

Extra Notes

Character Name

Eye Color

Also Known By

Hair Color

In Which Book Used

Hair Style

Major/Minor Character

Distinguishing Marks

Age

Height

Extra Notes

Weight

Build

Character Name

Also Known By

In Which Book Used

Major/Minor Character

Age

Height

Weight

Build

Eye Color

Hair Color

Hair Style

Distinguishing Marks

Extra Notes

Character Name

Also Known By

In Which Book Used

Major/Minor Character

Age

Height

Weight

Build

Eye Color

Hair Color

Hair Style

Distinguishing Marks

Extra Notes

Character Name

Also Known By

In Which Book Used

Major/Minor Character

Age

Height

Weight

Build

Eye Color

Hair Color

Hair Style

Distinguishing Marks

Extra Notes

Character Name

Also Known By

In Which Book Used

Major/Minor Character

Age

Height

Weight

Build

Eye Color

Hair Color

Hair Style

Distinguishing Marks

Extra Notes

Character Name

Eye Color

Also Known By

Hair Color

In Which Book Used

Hair Style

Major/Minor Character

Distinguishing Marks

Age

Height

Extra Notes

Weight

Build

Character Name

Also Known By

In Which Book Used

Major/Minor Character

Age

Height

Weight

Build

Eye Color

Hair Color

Hair Style

Distinguishing Marks

Extra Notes

| Character Name | Eye Color |

| Also Known By | Hair Color |

| In Which Book Used | Hair Style |

| Major/Minor Character | Distinguishing Marks |

| Age | |

| Height | Extra Notes |

| Weight | |

| Build | |

Character Name

Also Known By

In Which Book Used

Major/Minor Character

Age

Height

Weight

Build

Eye Color

Hair Color

Hair Style

Distinguishing Marks

Extra Notes

Character Name	Eye Color

Also Known By	Hair Color

In Which Book Used	Hair Style

Major/Minor Character	Distinguishing Marks

Age

Height

Weight

Build

Extra Notes

Character Name

Also Known By

In Which Book Used

Major/Minor Character

Age

Height

Weight

Build

Eye Color

Hair Color

Hair Style

Distinguishing Marks

Extra Notes

Character Name

Also Known By

In Which Book Used

Major/Minor Character

Age

Height

Weight

Build

Eye Color

Hair Color

Hair Style

Distinguishing Marks

Extra Notes

Character Name

Also Known By

In Which Book Used

Major/Minor Character

Age

Height

Weight

Build

Eye Color

Hair Color

Hair Style

Distinguishing Marks

Extra Notes

Character Name

Also Known By

In Which Book Used

Major/Minor Character

Age

Height

Weight

Build

Eye Color

Hair Color

Hair Style

Distinguishing Marks

Extra Notes

Character Name

Also Known By

In Which Book Used

Major/Minor Character

Age

Height

Weight

Build

Eye Color

Hair Color

Hair Style

Distinguishing Marks

Extra Notes

Character Name

Also Known By

In Which Book Used

Major/Minor Character

Age

Height

Weight

Build

Eye Color

Hair Color

Hair Style

Distinguishing Marks

Extra Notes

Character Name	Eye Color
Also Known By	Hair Color
In Which Book Used	Hair Style
Major/Minor Character	Distinguishing Marks
Age	
Height	Extra Notes
Weight	
Build	

Character Name	Eye Color
Also Known By	Hair Color
In Which Book Used	Hair Style
Major/Minor Character	Distinguishing Marks
Age	
Height	Extra Notes
Weight	
Build	

Character Name

Eye Color

Also Known By

Hair Color

In Which Book Used

Hair Style

Major/Minor Character

Distinguishing Marks

Age

Height

Extra Notes

Weight

Build

Character Name

Also Known By

In Which Book Used

Major/Minor Character

Age

Height

Weight

Build

Eye Color

Hair Color

Hair Style

Distinguishing Marks

Extra Notes

Character Name

Also Known By

In Which Book Used

Major/Minor Character

Age

Height

Weight

Build

Eye Color

Hair Color

Hair Style

Distinguishing Marks

Extra Notes

Character Name	Eye Color

Also Known By	Hair Color

In Which Book Used	Hair Style

Major/Minor Character	Distinguishing Marks

Age

Height

Weight

Build

Extra Notes

Character Name

Also Known By

In Which Book Used

Major/Minor Character

Age

Height

Weight

Build

Eye Color

Hair Color

Hair Style

Distinguishing Marks

Extra Notes

Character Name

Eye Color

Also Known By

Hair Color

In Which Book Used

Hair Style

Major/Minor Character

Distinguishing Marks

Age

Height

Extra Notes

Weight

Build

Character Name

Also Known By

In Which Book Used

Major/Minor Character

Age

Height

Weight

Build

Eye Color

Hair Color

Hair Style

Distinguishing Marks

Extra Notes

Character Name

Also Known By

In Which Book Used

Major/Minor Character

Age

Height

Weight

Build

Eye Color

Hair Color

Hair Style

Distinguishing Marks

Extra Notes

Character Name

Also Known By

In Which Book Used

Major/Minor Character

Age

Height

Weight

Build

Eye Color

Hair Color

Hair Style

Distinguishing Marks

Extra Notes

Character Name

Also Known By

In Which Book Used

Major/Minor Character

Age

Height

Weight

Build

Eye Color

Hair Color

Hair Style

Distinguishing Marks

Extra Notes

Character Name

Also Known By

In Which Book Used

Major/Minor Character

Age

Height

Weight

Build

Eye Color

Hair Color

Hair Style

Distinguishing Marks

Extra Notes

Character Name	Eye Color

Also Known By	Hair Color

In Which Book Used	Hair Style

Major/Minor Character	Distinguishing Marks

Age

Height

Weight

Build

Extra Notes

Character Name

Also Known By

In Which Book Used

Major/Minor Character

Age

Height

Weight

Build

Eye Color

Hair Color

Hair Style

Distinguishing Marks

Extra Notes

Character Name	Eye Color

Also Known By	Hair Color

In Which Book Used	Hair Style

Major/Minor Character	Distinguishing Marks

Age

Height

Weight

Build

Extra Notes

Character Name

Eye Color

Also Known By

Hair Color

In Which Book Used

Hair Style

Major/Minor Character

Distinguishing Marks

Age

Height

Weight

Extra Notes

Build

Character Name	Eye Color

Also Known By	Hair Color

In Which Book Used	Hair Style

Major/Minor Character	Distinguishing Marks

Age

Height

Weight

Build

Extra Notes

Character Name

Also Known By

In Which Book Used

Major/Minor Character

Age

Height

Weight

Build

Eye Color

Hair Color

Hair Style

Distinguishing Marks

Extra Notes

| Character Name | Eye Color |

| Also Known By | Hair Color |

| In Which Book Used | Hair Style |

| Major/Minor Character | Distinguishing Marks |

| Age | |

| Height | Extra Notes |

| Weight | |

| Build | |

Character Name

Eye Color

Also Known By

Hair Color

In Which Book Used

Hair Style

Major/Minor Character

Distinguishing Marks

Age

Height

Extra Notes

Weight

Build

Thank you so much for your purchase.

I really do hope that this book has helped you,
even in some small way.

Would you like to see different designs/styles?

I am always very happy to hear from customers,
so please feel free to email me on

teeceedesignstudio@yahoo.com

9 781673 490169